T0080889

Presented to:

_____

From:

_____

Date:

_____

Made in His Image
© 2020 by Zondervan

Requests for information should be addressed to:

Zondervan, 3900 Sparks Dr. SE, Grand Rapids, Michigan 49546

ISBN: 978-0-310-45382-6

Art direction: Patti Evans
Interior design: Kristy L. Edwards

Printed in China

19 20 21 22 23 24 HAHA 10 9 8 7 6 5 4 3 2 1

Made in His

Image

100 Bible Verses to Grow in Health and Wellness

1

I appeal to you therefore,
brothers, by the mercies of
God, to present your bodies
as a living sacrifice, holy and
acceptable to God, which
is your spiritual worship.

ROMANS 12:1 ESV

$\mathcal{E}$very day we are confronted with the topic of body image. Television commercials, advertisements, and magazine covers continually bombard our senses and not so subtly suggest what the ideal body should look like. But the Bible assigns greater worth to the body than mere physical appearance. The Bible represents the body as God's creation (Genesis 1:27). As a response to God's goodness, we are to present our bodies to Him as an act of worship. All human beings are created in the image of God, and that reality gives every person great significance. While it's important that we take good care of our bodies, if we focus exclusively on our appearance, we miss the most important point. Presenting our bodies to God as a living sacrifice is at the heart of spiritual worship. Our bodies were not made to be worshiped, but rather our bodies were made to worship God.

> *God, thank You for my body. Give me wisdom to take good care of it, and teach me what it means to offer it to You as an act of spiritual worship.*

2

We are God's workmanship,
created in Christ Jesus
to do good works,
which God prepared in
advance for us to do.

EPHESIANS 2:10 NIV

*M*ost of us have at least one thing we don't like about our bodies, and if we aren't careful, it's easy to become obsessed with our perceived flaws. But have you ever pondered the fact that you are God's workmanship? When the apostle Paul wrote his letter to the church at Ephesus, he spoke of humankind as being God's "workmanship" (Ephesians 2:10 NIV). The term *workmanship* comes from the Greek word *poiema*, which is where we get the word *poem*.[1] When we live the way God designed us to function, we are literally God's poetry to the world. Paul communicated that God created human beings as His workmanship for the purpose of good works. Of course, our good works don't have the power to save us. The Scriptures teach that we are saved by grace through faith (Ephesians 2:8–9). But good works are a by-product of our salvation. Without good works, we miss our calling.

> *Jesus, You created me to live with purpose, and I am Your workmanship. Empower me to live in such a way that I am God's poetry to the world.*

3

God has not given us a spirit
of fear, but of power and of
love and of a sound mind.

2 TIMOTHY 1:7

God created human beings in such a way that our bodies, souls, and minds are closely connected. For better or worse, our thoughts have a profound impact on our bodies. It is possible to literally worry ourselves sick. Some research suggests that three out of four doctor visits are caused by stress-related illnesses.[2] God knew that worry and stress would be a chronic problem for His people, and the Bible is not silent about the issue. The Scriptures teach that fear doesn't come from God (2 Timothy 1:7). On the contrary, He has given us the tools to manage our thoughts and live in His peace. The Bible teaches that if we are believers in Jesus Christ, then the Holy Spirit dwells in us. God's people have the ability to rely on the Holy Spirit's presence, which brings a spirit of power, love, and a sound mind. The key is being mindful of His presence and trusting His promises.

Father, thank You for giving me the ability to live in peace. Help me to use the tools You have given me to live by faith and to reject fear.

4

God created human
beings in his image. In
the image of God he
created them. He created
them male and female.

GENESIS 1:27 NCV

S ome of us spend an enormous amount of time and effort attempting to prove our self-worth. A constant need to be validated impacts our work, home life, finances, fitness, and every aspect of day-to-day living. When we lack understanding of our self-worth, our efforts to excel aren't motivated by the desire to do our best with our God-given potential, but rather, they are fueled by insecurity to prove we are enough. It's an exhausting and unnecessary predicament. As God's people, our value isn't decided by society. Our value stems from the reality that we are created in God's image (Genesis 1:27). Our accomplishments or lack of them don't assign our value. God defines us and deems us valuable. This reality should influence how we see ourselves, and it should impact how we treat other people. All people are created in the image of God, and therefore every person should be treated with kindness and dignity.

> *Father, I am honored to be created in Your image. My worth is found in You alone. Give me eyes that see Your image in all people, and help me treat others in a way that honors You.*

5

Since we are surrounded
by so great a cloud of
witnesses, let us also lay
aside every weight, and sin
which clings so closely, and
let us run with endurance the
race that is set before us.

HEBREWS 12:1 ESV

*A*ll of us need motivation. When we consider our goals, hopes, and dreams, it's beneficial for us to have other people to look to as examples. The author of Hebrews wrote to an audience who was faced with the risk of being persecuted for their faith and needed encouragement. In Hebrews 11, the chapter known as the Hall of Faith, the writer included a long list of people who had lived by faith and brought glory to God. The writer brought attention to these saints from the past so readers would be encouraged and follow their example. None of the people mentioned were without flaws, because no human being is perfect, and we all sin. But there are plenty of people we can look to and learn from. We find them in the pages of Scripture and in our local churches. The apostle Paul said, "Be imitators of me, as I am of Christ" (1 Corinthians 11:1 ESV). To flourish in our faith, we need mature Christians to look to as an example.

> *Lord, thank You for mature believers who set a godly example for me to follow. Lead me to these people in my church and community. As I grow, help me to be an example to others.*

6

Do you not know that
your bodies are temples
of the Holy Spirit, who is
in you, whom you have
received from God?

1 CORINTHIANS 6:19 NIV

The Bible teaches that all Christians are indwelled by the Holy Spirit. As Christians, our bodies are no longer our own, because we were bought with the blood of Christ. In response, the Scriptures instruct us to glorify God with our bodies (1 Corinthians 6:20). Every believer in Jesus Christ is, in a real sense, God's temple. A temple exists to be a place for worship to glorify God. The apostle Paul instructed Christians to live lives of sexual purity because to sin in our bodies is to sin in God's sanctuary. "For [we] are the temple of the living God" (2 Corinthians 6:16). When we are mindful that our bodies are indwelled by the Holy Spirit, it should motivate us to seek God's grace to live in a way that is holy and pleasing to Him. At any given time, the living God is as close to us as our next breath. If we are mindful of His presence, we will seek deeper purity and increased holiness.

Lord, thank You for making my body Your temple. Sanctify me so I grow in purity and increase in holiness. Make me strong in the places I am weak.

7

Whatever you do, do it
heartily, as to the Lord
and not to men.

COLOSSIANS 3:23

*I*n Scripture, the first thing God reveals to us about His character is that He is working (Genesis 1). As His image bearers, God's people are to be productive members of society. Our homes and communities should be better because we are in them. It doesn't matter if we are called to be stay-at-home parents, full-time employees, students, or volunteers; the Bible instructs Christians to give our best effort to every task. In today's scripture, Paul instructed his readers to work hard with the mind-set of working for the Lord and not men. In other words, Christians are to approach every task as if they are doing it for Jesus. We all know people who do the bare minimum. That should never be the case for God's people. Christ-followers should be the hardest-working people in their homes and places of employment. We have motivation to do so. Paul wrote, "[Know] that from the Lord you will receive the reward of the inheritance; for you serve the Lord Christ" (Colossians 3:24).

Lord, give me the strength, energy, and motivation to approach every task as if I am working for You. Help me always to do my best and to have an excellent work ethic.

8

"Life is more than
food, and the body is
more than clothes."

LUKE 12:23 NCV

*W*orry robs us of valuable energy. When we are consumed with worry, we are distracted and often lose priceless time contemplating things that may never happen. The Bible warns against worry and instructs Christians to avoid it. One of the primary things we worry about is having enough. Possessing ample food and clothing is a legitimate concern, but Jesus told His disciples there was more to life than food and clothes (Luke 12:23). Jesus directed the disciples' attention to the Father's character: "Look at the birds. They don't plant or harvest, they don't have storerooms or barns, but God feeds them. And you are worth much more than birds" (v. 24 NCV). At its core, worry is an issue of faith. When we trust God to provide for our needs, we are free to focus our energy, time, and resources on cultivating a growing faith and living a life that brings glory to God.

> *Father, I don't want my life to be characterized by worry. Please provide for my needs. Help me to focus my energy on the tasks You have called me to and avoid wasting energy.*

9

You were bought with a price.
So glorify God in your body.

1 CORINTHIANS 6:20 ESV

Most of us measure the value of things in currency and assign worth in terms of dollars and cents. But spiritually speaking, there are countless things that can't be measured in that manner. In today's reading Paul was reminding Christians we were bought with a price, so we are to glorify God with our bodies. If we think in terms of financial currency, we will vastly underestimate the cost of our redemption. The apostle Peter wrote that we were ransomed, "not with perishable things such as silver or gold, but with the precious blood of Christ" (1 Peter 1:18–19 ESV). Our redemption was so costly it demanded the blood of the sinless Son of God. It's a staggering thought, isn't it? But Jesus willingly paid that costly sum. A Christian's worth can never be estimated in dollars and cents. Our worth was settled at Calvary when Jesus paid the ultimate price for our redemption.

Lord, thank You for being willing to pay the highest price possible for my redemption. Increase my wisdom so I know how to honor You with my body. Help me to remember You alone define my worth.

10

He gives strength
to the weary
and increases the
power of the weak.

ISAIAH 40:29 NIV

The demands of day-to-day living have the potential to leave us running on fumes. Our fast-paced work lives, exercise regimens, and overbooked schedules leave little time for rest and reflection. In some instances, personal loss, depression and anxiety, and the impact of living in a fallen world get us down. But the Bible reveals that God replenishes His people's strength and gives us everything we need to fulfill our responsibilities. As Christians, we don't have to muster up our own resources and energy. Instead, we have the opportunity to approach God and ask Him to give us the strength and power we lack. Living by faith means we trust God to keep His promises, and in doing so we move forward clinging to the assurance that God will do for us what we cannot do for ourselves. God possesses infinite resources of strength and power, and we can be confident He will keep us going.

> *Father, thank You for Your willingness to provide everything I lack. When I am weary, please increase my strength. I will move forward in faith with confidence that You will provide.*

11

Charm is deceitful and
beauty is passing,
but a woman who fears the
Lᴏʀᴅ, she shall be praised.

PROVERBS 31:30

It's no secret that the media puts an excessive emphasis on personal appearance. Heavily edited and airbrushed photographs of ultrathin models impose a false reality and unrealistic expectations on those of us living in the real world. But there are far more important qualities than physical beauty. In today's passage, the writer of Proverbs was informing readers that charm is misleading, and even the most beautiful people will lose their good looks. Our culture seldom speaks about the value of our spiritual lives, but the book of Proverbs notes that a woman who reveres the Lord shall be praised. If we live long enough, it's inevitable that our appearance will diminish with age. But our relationship with God has the potential to grow more vibrant with each passing year. That relationship is something we will enjoy throughout eternity. With this truth in mind, we should invest our time and efforts on earth accordingly.

> *God, help me to remember my relationship with You is the most important thing. Teach me to prioritize what is most valuable. I revere You above all things.*

12

It is God who arms
me with strength,
and makes my way perfect.

PSALM 18:32

*H*ave you ever been faced with overwhelming obstacles and mounting opposition? Psalms has plenty to say about facing adversity. God had promised David he would be the king of Israel, but there was a long season before David took the throne when it seemed as if the opposition would overwhelm him. In a fit of rage and jealousy, King Saul and his men were in hot pursuit of David, with the intention of killing him. These enemies were too much for David to handle, but God intervened on David's behalf and saved him. David took no credit for his deliverance. He knew it was God who had provided him with the strength he needed to escape the hand of Saul, and it was God who guided him on the right path. We all go through seasons when we are confronted with obstacles that are too much for us to handle. When we do, there is no need to panic. God's children have the privilege of relying on His resources.

Father, nothing is too hard for You. Give me the confidence to persevere during hard times. When I face obstacles, teach me to rely on Your resources and not my own.

13

Do not be wise in
your own eyes;
fear the Lᴏʀᴅ and
depart from evil.
It will be health to your flesh,
and strength to your bones.

PROVERBS 3:7–8

Often, we think we know what is best for us, but if our belief system is contrary to God's Word, we've gotten off track. God created us, and He knows what is best for us. The Scriptures are the primary way God communicates with us and teaches us how to live a godly life. In today's passage, the author of Proverbs reminded readers to avoid thinking we are wiser than God's commands. A life of sinful disobedience is detrimental to every area of our life, including our physical health. Wisdom calls for us to do things God's way. The good news is that when we obey God and His commandments, we thrive spiritually, and it's even good for our bodies. Avoiding evil and living a godly lifestyle are "health to [our] flesh and strength to [our] bones." (Proverbs 3:8). Obedience sometimes seems painful, but it ultimately brings blessing, and it is the best way to live.

> *Father, teach me to trust Your ways more than I trust my own. Help me to live a life of obedience that impacts every aspect of my life for the better.*

14

Do you not know that those who run in a race all run, but one receives the prize? Run in such a way that you may obtain it.

1 CORINTHIANS 9:24

The apostle Paul often used sports metaphors to describe the Christian life. In his first letter to the church at Corinth, he compared the Christian life to a runner in a race. Paul pointed out that there are several runners in the race, but only one can win. In the Christian life, we don't compete against one another, but we must confront obstacles that have the potential to make us stumble in our faith journey. We each have to run our own race and set aside things that hinder our spiritual growth. In the Christian life, there should be progress. God did not create us to be stagnant, and we should continually increase in knowledge. There is an expectation that we will mature in our faith. In the same way an athlete prepares for an event by challenging his or her body, Christ-followers are to train in righteousness by engaging in spiritual disciplines, such as Bible study, worship, and prayer.

Father, I want to grow in my faith and spiritual maturity. Make me aware of obstacles that hinder my growth. Give me the desire to commit to a lifestyle of engaging in spiritual disciplines that help me to mature spiritually.

15

Those who wait on the Lord
shall renew their strength;
they shall mount up with
wings like eagles,
they shall run and
not be weary,
they shall walk and not faint.

ISAIAH 40:31

$\mathcal{H}$ave you ever experienced a long season of waiting? No one likes to wait, but the Scriptures make it clear that God routinely calls on His people to wait. When we are waiting for a change in a specific situation, it can be both discouraging and exhausting. But if we focus our thoughts on God while we wait, instead of on our circumstances, we will be renewed and replenished. Waiting with our eyes fixed on God rather than our situation is a small change of focus that makes a huge impact. In today's passage, the prophet Isaiah communicated to his readers that God renews our strength as we wait and provides us with the energy to soar like an eagle. Time and again we will find ourselves in circumstances that force us to wait on God. Learning to adjust our focus and keep our eyes fixed on Him will make our times of waiting replenishing rather than exhausting.

> *Father, in seasons of waiting, teach me to fix my eyes on You. Renew my energy so I can do everything You call me to do.*

16

The Lord God is my strength;
He will make my feet
like deer's feet,
and He will make me
walk on my high hills.

HABAKKUK 3:19

$\mathcal{A}$merican culture puts a heavy emphasis on self-confidence, and we frequently hear people tell each other things like, "You've got this." But relying on our own strength is a mistake that will leave us sorely disappointed. Simply put, we all come up against things that are too hard for us. But nothing is too hard for God. As Christians, we aren't called to live in our strength. The Bible teaches we must rely on God's infinite strength and power. The prophet Habakkuk understood his own limitations, and that's why he said, "The LORD God is my strength" (Habakkuk 3:19). When we rely on God's infinite power, rather than our resources, there is no limit to what is possible. If we rely on our own strength, our experiences will be limited. But if we trust God to be our strength, we will live extraordinary lives that bring glory to God.

> *Lord, I confess I have no strength or power apart from You. Teach me to rely on Your strength and not my own. My confidence is in You.*

17

"Love the Lord your God
with all your heart, all
your soul, all your mind,
and all your strength."

MARK 12:30 NCV

One day Jesus was talking to a group of people when one of the scribes asked Jesus which of the commandments was the most important. Jesus told the crowd that loving God with everything you have is the most important command, and that loving other people was the second most important (Mark 12:30–31). Loving God impacts everything. Our love for God will motivate us to obey Him, and as a result, we will make wise choices that align with His will. When we love God, we obey Him because we want to, not because we feel we have to. A love for God allows us to have an intimate relationship with Christ that is personal, rather than just dry religion. If we lack love for God, it's wise to ask Him to give us a heart that loves Him above all things. And the more time we spend reading the Bible and coming to understand God's character and ways, the more we will grow in our love for Him.

Father, I want to love You more than anything else. Give me a heart that treasures You above all things.

18

I can do all things through
him who strengthens me.

PHILIPPIANS 4:13 ESV

When the apostle Paul wrote his letter to the church at Philippi, he was in prison for preaching the gospel. Since the beginning of the early church, it has not been uncommon for Christians to suffer for their faith, but Paul suffered more than most. He was imprisoned, beaten, stoned, shipwrecked, lost at sea, in constant danger, hungry, and exposed to harsh circumstances, all because he was sharing the gospel (2 Corinthians 11:23–27). Paul even said that he was so burdened beyond his strength that he despaired of life, but he knew it was to teach him to rely on God rather than himself (2 Corinthians 1:8–9). Despite his circumstances, Paul had good reason to be optimistic, because he knew he could rely on Christ's strength and accomplish whatever He called him to. Paul's message remains true for us today. We are called to rely on Jesus, who will give us everything we need to persevere.

> *Jesus, thank You for giving me the strength to do what I can't do on my own. Direct my thoughts to Your ever-present help and sustaining grace.*

19

The light of the eyes
rejoices the heart,
and a good report makes
the bones healthy.

PROVERBS 15:30

It's impossible to live a positive life if we have a negative attitude. Ultimately, we are the only ones who can control our attitudes, but our attitudes are heavily influenced by the people we spend the most time with. If we are constantly surrounded by people who expect the worst in every situation and talk poorly about other people, it will have a negative impact on us. The book of Proverbs often speaks about wisdom and making good choices. In today's passage, the writer reminded his readers that "a good report makes the bones healthy" (Proverbs 15:30). In other words, a good word makes a positive impact on our physical health. While we can't always completely control who we spend time with, we can choose to have a good attitude and speak in a positive manner. It's wise to surround ourselves with people who have faith and possess hopeful anticipation. Constant negativity is a trait we want to avoid, but having a positive attitude is a choice we can make for ourselves.

God, as Your child I have every reason to have a positive attitude. Transform all negativity in my attitude and help me to see the good in every situation.

20

Take for yourself wheat,
barley, beans, lentils, millet,
and spelt; put them into
one vessel, and make bread
of them for yourself.

EZEKIEL 4:9

God designed our bodies in such a way that they need proper nutrition to function at an optimum level. Thankfully, God also provided us with food sources that nourish our bodies. If we constantly feed our bodies junk food, it's likely we will be poorly nourished and low on energy. It's common knowledge that large amounts of processed foods harm our physical health, and most experts agree these foods have the potential to cause a number of diseases. Our souls, bodies, and minds are closely connected, and as a result, our food choices affect each area. Healthy food in its most natural state will nourish our bodies, and when eaten in proper amounts will help us maintain a healthy weight. God assigned each of us to be stewards of our bodies. Part of good stewardship is making the right food choices that enable us to function at the highest level.

Father, please help me make wise choices about food. I recognize those choices impact every aspect of my life. Teach me to value my body and be a good steward.

21

You are my lamp, O Lᴏʀᴅ;
the Lᴏʀᴅ shall enlighten
my darkness.
For by You I can run
against a troop;
by my God I can
leap over a wall.

2 SAMUEL 22:29–30

*a*t some point all of us have experienced situations where we lacked confidence. Perhaps it was a fitness goal, an assignment at work, a project at school, a situation at home, or a medical problem we were facing. King David was no stranger to fear and daunting circumstances. After a time of severe hardship, the Lord delivered David from the hand of his enemies and King Saul. Interestingly, at the time of his victory, David didn't celebrate all the ways he conquered his fears or grew in self-confidence. Instead, David acknowledged what God had done on his behalf. David's harrowing circumstances taught him that God was his strength and provision. Rather than becoming increasingly self-confident, David grew in faith in God's provision. As we approach daunting tasks and scary circumstances, we must remember God is everything we need Him to be. The goal is not for us to grow more self-confident but to increase in faith in the God who can never fail us.

Father, help me to grow in confidence in Your faith and provision. When I am confronted with circumstances that scare me, teach me to place my faith in You.

22

I have taught you in
the way of wisdom;
I have led you in right paths.
When you walk, your steps
will not be hindered,
and when you run, you
will not stumble.
Take firm hold of
instruction, do not let go;
keep her, for she is your life.

PROVERBS 4:11–13

No one wants to be foolish. The Bible speaks of the way of the wise and the way of the fool, and thankfully, we all have the opportunity to grow in wisdom. Wisdom gives us the ability to know the best way to proceed in any given situation and to apply the truths of Scripture to our daily lives. The apostle James encouraged his readers to ask God for more wisdom: "If any of you lacks wisdom, let him ask of God, who gives to all liberally and without reproach, and it will be given to him" (James 1:5). If we want to make good choices and thrive in our faith, we must continually pursue wisdom. God has given us permission to ask Him to increase our wisdom, and as we study the Scriptures, we will grow in wisdom and increase in insight. In the Christian life, the pursuit of wisdom is a lifelong goal.

Father, please give me wisdom in every area of my life. Teach me to seek wisdom through prayer and Your Word. Help me to apply the truths of Scripture to my daily decisions.

23

I do not run without a
goal. I fight like a boxer
who is hitting something—
not just the air.

1 CORINTHIANS 9:26 NCV

When we're trying to get in shape, if we aren't careful, it's easy to drift from day to day and week to week with no defined goals. Before we know it, months pass, and we haven't made any progress in our health. The apostle Paul knew it was important for God's people to set goals in their spiritual lives. In today's passage, he compared the Christian life to a boxer who aims for a target. As Christians, we should prayerfully set goals and then define a plan to achieve them. Have you ever considered setting a goal to read through the Bible in a year? Or set a specific time each day for prayer? Perhaps you want to get in better physical shape or make healthier food choices. Regardless of what it is you are trying to accomplish, it's wise to name a goal and then plan how to make it happen. As we make goals, we should seek God in prayer and ask for His wisdom in how to proceed. None of us will ever drift toward spiritual maturity. If we want to grow in our faith, we need to set goals that lead us toward growth.

> *Father, I want to set goals that honor You and help me reach my potential. Give me wisdom to set good goals and the self-control to achieve them.*

24

While bodily training is of
some value, godliness is of
value in every way, as it holds
promise for the present life
and also for the life to come.

1 TIMOTHY 4:8 ESV

espite widespread research that supports the claim that exercise is beneficial to the body and is successful at preventing many diseases, few people get the recommended amount of daily exercise. One report claims that less than 5 percent of adults get the recommended thirty minutes per day of exercise, and only one in three meet the weekly recommendations.[3] In Paul's letter to his protégé, Timothy, he mentioned that bodily training or exercise is of value. God has provided us with a way to keep our bodies in good shape, to lower our risk for illness, and to improve our mood. Exercise is a good investment of time. But Paul also communicated to Timothy that while exercise is of "some value" (1 Timothy 4:8 ESV), godliness is valuable in every way. It's possible for us to work our physical bodies into peak condition, but if we ignore our spiritual health, we will suffer. Thankfully, we don't have to choose one or the other but can pursue both.

Father, teach me to care for both my body and my soul. Give me the self-discipline to engage in physical conditioning and soul care. Help me not to neglect either one.

25

She girds herself
with strength,
and strengthens her arms.

PROVERBS 31:17

od has given us one body, built to last a lifetime. Unfortunately, when humanity fell, disease and illness became part of the human experience and impacted our bodies (Genesis 3). Thankfully, there are steps we can take to lessen the blow that living in a fallen world has on our bodies. When the writer of Proverbs described a virtuous woman, he mentioned that she "girds herself with strength, and strengthens her arms" (31:17). To function at maximum capacity, it's beneficial to stay in the best shape possible. Physical fitness isn't simply a matter of vanity; it's a matter of keeping our bodies in optimum condition so we can fulfill our callings and live with vibrancy. Undoubtedly, if we live long enough, we will all be affected by aging and have medical issues arise. But if we make wise choices in regard to diet, nutrition, and exercise, we have the potential to avoid some problems and enjoy healthy bodies for as long as possible.

Lord, I pray You will help me to stay physically fit and active. Help me to take good care of my body so I can fulfill my calling and function at an optimum level.

26

The LORD will guide
you continually,
and satisfy your
soul in drought,
and strengthen your bones;
you shall be like a
watered garden,
and like a spring of water,
whose waters do not fail.

ISAIAH 58:11

$\int$ f you've been a Christian very long, there's a good chance you've experienced a time of spiritual dryness. We all go through times when we struggle in our Bible reading, wonder if our prayers are being heard, and don't feel as close to the Lord as we would prefer. In today's passage, the prophet Isaiah reminded his readers that God is faithful to guide us back on the right path and satisfy our soul during times of drought, even strengthening our bones (Isaiah 58:11). There were times when even King David felt forgotten by God: "How long O LORD? Will you forget me forever? How long will You hide Your face from me?" (Psalm 13:1). During times of spiritual dryness, we must keep engaging in prayer and Bible study, and like David, continue communicating with God in our despair. Times of spiritual dryness are never pleasant, but they don't last forever. When our intimacy with the Lord returns, it will be sweeter than it was before, and we will appreciate it all the more.

Lord, I desperately want to have an intimate relationship with You. Allow me to sense Your presence in prayer and reveal Yourself to me through Your Scriptures.

27

So whether you eat or drink
or whatever you do, do it
all for the glory of God.

1 CORINTHIANS 10:31 NIV

The goal of the Christian life is to bring glory to God. But we are mistaken if we believe we only bring glory to God in the context of "spiritual things." Certainly we do bring glory to God in the midst of church life, service, and things we typically associate with God's glory. But in the apostle Paul's first letter to the church at Corinth, he communicated that a Christian can bring glory to God in the ordinary things of life, like eating or drinking (1 Corinthians 10:31). If we aren't careful, we tend to compartmentalize what we consider to be the "spiritual" versus "non-spiritual." But the reality is, everything we do either honors or dishonors God. If we belong to Jesus, then every aspect of our life is to be committed to His glory.

Jesus, teach me to invest every day of my life in a way that brings glory to You. Help me to use even the mundane things to communicate that I belong to You and You are worthy of all glory.

28

Wise people have
great power,
and those with knowledge
have great strength.

PROVERBS 24:5 NCV

*T*o flourish in our spiritual lives, we must continue to grow in wisdom and knowledge. One of the messages of the book of Proverbs is that we can't thrive without the help of other people. Wise people learn from others, even when counsel comes in the form of correction. The writer of Proverbs went on to say, "You need advice when you go to war. If you have lots of good advice, you will win" (24:6 NCV). The writer was saying that we need more than strength to win our battles. Most of us won't go to war in a literal sense, but we will face uphill battles that challenge us. In tough times, we need strength, but we also need wisdom, knowledge, counsel, and guidance. It's essential for us to have a few godly people we trust and can go to for advice. We all have blind spots that we can't see, and it's crucial to have the input of mature believers who can help us make the best choices.

> *Father, teach me to continually seek increased wisdom and knowledge. I ask You to give me godly friends who are wise and willing to provide me with counsel.*

29

No discipline seems pleasant
at the time, but painful. Later
on, however, it produces
a harvest of righteousness
and peace for those who
have been trained by it.
Therefore, strengthen your
feeble arms and weak knees.

HEBREWS 12:11–12 NIV

Whether we're engaged in a fitness routine, going back to school, or working toward any number of other worthy goals, self-discipline is essential if we want to experience success. Naturally, none of us enjoy the process. But to accomplish anything of value, we must learn to discipline ourselves in the present so we can enjoy the payoff in the future. To be self-disciplined, we must be willing to tell ourselves no and manage our impulses. If we always do exactly what we want to do when we want to do it, we will never make any progress toward our goals. Whether we are attempting a Bible reading plan, an exercise program, healthier eating, or a big project at work, our goals will demand self-discipline. Thankfully, one of the fruits of the Spirit is self-control (Galatians 5:22–23). It's wise to pray and ask God to increase our self-control and then move forward in faith knowing we have what we need.

> *Father, please increase my ability to control my impulses and increase my self-discipline. Teach me to manage my thoughts and do what I need to hit my goals.*

30

But the fruit of the
Spirit is love, joy, peace,
longsuffering, kindness,
goodness, faithfulness,
gentleness, and self-control.

GALATIANS 5:22–23

When we are feeling sick or suffering from an injury, we can go to the doctor and have tests run, and there's a good chance the doctor can determine a diagnosis. There are no diagnostic tests for our spiritual lives, but there are symptoms that give us clues as to what's going on. The Bible teaches that at any given point we are walking either in the spirit or in the flesh (Romans 8:5). The apostle Paul went on to say that to set our minds on the flesh is death, but to set our minds on the Spirit is life and peace (v. 6). Following our flesh will lead us to sin. But when we are submitted to the will of God and walking by the guidance of the Holy Spirit, we will experience increased measures of love, joy, peace, longsuffering, kindness, goodness, faithfulness, gentleness, and self-control.

Father, I want to walk in the Spirit. Help me to be swift to repent when I am influenced by my flesh and to submit to the promptings of the Spirit quickly.

31

All things are lawful for me,
but all things are not helpful.
All things are lawful for me,
but I will not be brought
under the power of any.

1 CORINTHIANS 6:12

The grace of Christ provides Christians with freedom, but we need to be wise with the margin of freedom we have. Paul insisted that he wouldn't be mastered by anyone or anything but Jesus. There are countless things that aren't considered "sinful" but still have the potential to enslave us. For instance, food, social media, relationships, money, and possessions all have the potential to be great blessings to us. But if they are consumed or pursued in a way that is unhealthy, they can be unhelpful or even toxic to our souls. God intends for His people to be free from all things that enslave us. Paul wrote, "Sin shall not have dominion over you, for you are not under law but under grace" (Romans 6:14). Just because something is permissible doesn't necessarily mean it is the best choice. We need to consider our habits prayerfully and refuse to be enslaved to them.

Father, I ask for discernment in making good decisions about my habits. Give me wisdom to avoid anything that will enslave me to sin or limit the freedom that Christ has provided for me.

32

Do not get drunk with wine,
for that is debauchery, but
be filled with the Spirit.

EPHESIANS 5:18 ESV

*S*ome people believe the Bible calls for Christians to completely abstain from drinking alcohol, while others believe the Bible doesn't forbid alcohol entirely but does forbid drunkenness. Today's reading clearly warns that drunkenness leads to poor choices. Instead, the apostle Paul wrote, we should "be filled with the Spirit" (Ephesians 5:18 ESV). The phrase "be filled" comes from the Greek word *pleroo* and literally means "keep being filled."[4] At the time of our salvation, we are "sealed" with the Holy Spirit, and that sealing is permanent (Ephesians 1:13). But to live in the full measure of the Spirit, we need to keep being filled, and that calls for us to confess our sin, submit to the Spirit's control, obey the Scriptures, and live with a continual mindfulness of the personal presence of Christ.

Father, teach me to be continually filled with the Spirit. Help me to be quick to confess and repent of my sins, to live in obedience to Your Word, and to be continually aware of Your presence.

33

I will praise You, for
I am fearfully and
wonderfully made:
marvelous are Your works,
and that my soul
knows very well.

PSALM 139:14

*A*s we age, we realize our bodies don't look or feel the same way they did when we are young. But if we take time to contemplate the intricate way God created the human body, we will be amazed. The body is a complex system that really is a marvel. In today's reading, the psalmist expressed praise to God for the way He designed our bodies. There are countless ways we take our bodies for granted, and we don't realize how many things are consistently going right in our body until something goes wrong. When was the last time you thanked God for your eyesight or hearing? Have you ever wondered how different your life would be without proper brain function, memory, or the ability to speak? Rather than contemplating all the things we'd like to change about our bodies, let us praise God for all the ways our bodies serve us.

> *Father, I marvel at the way You designed the human body. Thank You for all the ways my body serves me well. Help me to take good care of it and view it as a gift from You.*

34

Have you found honey? Eat only as much as you need.

PROVERBS 25:16

$\mathcal{G}$od has provided us with many things to enjoy, and among those things is delicious food. God made food to eat that is good for us and pleasing to our palates. But today's passage teaches that moderation is key. This is an area many of us struggle with. One poll revealed that more than two-thirds of Americans are overweight or obese.[5] Most of us know that obesity is a threat to our health. To complicate matters, eating too much of the wrong foods leaves us nutritionally malnourished even if we are overweight. A well-balanced diet filled with healthy foods helps us have the most energy and feel our best. That doesn't mean we have to avoid our favorite foods entirely, but the Scriptures teach we need to practice moderation. When we practice temperance in our eating habits, our bodies will be healthier, and when we do eat our favorite foods, it will be even more enjoyable.

Father, thank You for creating food that is desirable to eat and nutritious for my body. Help me to show self-control in my eating habits and approach all things with moderation.

35

The LORD said to Samuel,
". . . the LORD does not
look at the things people
look at. People look at the
outward appearance, but the
LORD looks at the heart."

1 SAMUEL 16:7 NIV

You've probably heard the old cliché, "You can't judge a book by its cover." The point is, appearances can be deceiving. The Lord had ordered the prophet Samuel to go to the house of Jesse to seek out a replacement for King Saul. Initially, Samuel believed Jesse's son Eliab to be God's chosen replacement for Saul, but God rejected Eliab and six of his brothers. God instructed Samuel to disregard outward appearance, because He was concerned with the heart (1 Samuel 16:7). David was a shepherd and the youngest of Jesse's sons. It was evident that Jesse didn't believe David would be chosen, but God chose David to be the king of Israel. God didn't make His choice based on outward appearance, but referred to David as a man after His own heart (Acts 13:22). Many times we are more concerned with our appearance than with the state of our hearts. But God cares far more about our hearts than how we look.

God, I want a heart that is fully devoted to You. Teach me to focus more on the heart and less on outward appearance.

36

"Fear not, for I am with you;
be not dismayed, for
I am your God.
I will strengthen You,
yes, I will help you,
I will uphold you with My
righteous right hand."

ISAIAH 41:10

Fear has a negative impact on our minds and bodies and is something we need to keep in check. In Scripture, when God instructed His people not to fear, He followed up with the assurance, "for I am with you" (Isaiah 41:10). Undoubtedly, there will be times we are confronted with legitimate fears. Life in a fallen world means there is the possibility of medical issues, financial concerns, relationship problems, losing loved ones, and a variety of other things that give us good reason to be afraid. We will never conquer our fears trying to convince ourselves there is no reason to be fearful. In today's passage, God doesn't tell us there is no reason to be afraid. He tells us not to be fearful or dismayed because He is our God, and He is present to help. We can confront our fear head-on when we are mindful that God is with us and that He is more powerful than anything we will ever face.

Father, thank You for always being with me. Help me remember that You are more powerful than any problem and that You provide the strength I need in every circumstance.

37

Do not worry about anything,
but pray and ask God for
everything you need, always
giving thanks. And God's
peace, which is so great
we cannot understand it,
will keep your hearts and
minds in Christ Jesus.

PHILIPPIANS 4:6–7 NCV

*E*very day millions of people waste valuable energy by worrying. Worry can emotionally and physically drain us, and it has zero potential to influence our lives for the better.

The apostle Paul was especially fond of the church at Philippi (Philippians 1:3, 7). In his letter to the Philippians, he provided his readers with the prescription for worry. Paul instructed them to replace worry with prayer. Praying about our concerns and giving thanks for all the ways God has blessed us shifts our focus from our situation to the God who is able to address any problem. Not only is it appropriate to give thanks to God, but gratitude readjusts our thought processes, reminds us of all the ways God has been good to us, and increases our faith that God will again act on our behalf. Worrying can't change our circumstances, but prayer can move mountains (Mark 11:23–24).

Lord, when I am tempted to worry, give me a stronger desire to take my concerns to You in prayer. Remind me of all the ways You have blessed me, and teach me to focus on You rather than on my problems.

38

Be strong in the Lord and
in the strength of his might.
Put on the whole armor
of God, that you may be
able to stand against the
schemes of the devil.

EPHESIANS 6:10–11 ESV

When it comes to the subject of the devil, people tend to make one of two mistakes. Either they worry incessantly and become paralyzed with fear, or they entirely ignore the threat and become an easy target. Neither extreme is desirable. Jesus warned His followers that we have an enemy who is committed to our destruction (John 10:10). Ignoring the reality is foolish. But Jesus hasn't left us without help. In today's reading, the apostle Paul described the armor of God, which protects the Christian in spiritual warfare. We are to put on the whole armor of God so we can stand against the schemes of the devil. Although we have a strong foe, there is no reason for us to live in fear. The apostle John assured his readers, "He who is in you is greater than he who is in the world" (1 John 4:4).

> *Jesus, help me be mindful that I have an enemy who is committed to my destruction. Teach me to put on the whole armor of God so that I can stand against the plans of the Enemy.*

39

No temptation has overtaken
you except what is common
to mankind. And God is
faithful; he will not let you
be tempted beyond what
you can bear. But when
you are tempted, he will
also provide a way out so
that you can endure it.

1 CORINTHIANS 10:13 NIV

When we are facing temptation, it's common to feel alone and as if we are the only one struggling. But in today's passage, the scripture makes clear that we all struggle with sin and we haven't been tempted in a way that others haven't experienced. No temptation is unique to us, and we can rest assured that millions of other people have experienced the same temptation. The Bible also assures us that God will not allow His children to be tempted more than what we can withstand, and when we are struggling with temptation, He will provide a way for us to prevail. Jesus was tempted in every way and yet was without sin (Hebrews 4:15). Because He understands the nature and intensity of temptation, we can approach Him in our time of need, and He will provide us an escape from it.

> *Lord, when I am tempted, give me the power to resist sin. In times of temptation, I pray I will be quick to seek Jesus' mercy and grace.*

40

Do not mix with winebibbers,
or with gluttonous
eaters of meat;
for the drunkard and the
glutton will come to poverty,
and drowsiness will clothe
a man with rags.

PROVERBS 23:20–21

We will never have a healthy mind-set if we are constantly surrounded by toxic people. The people closest to us have an enormous influence on our thinking. When we spend time with people, we tend to pick up their habits, mannerisms, and attitudes. Today's Bible reading warns us to avoid people who aren't able to practice self-control, because their actions will negatively impact their future. That doesn't mean we shouldn't extend grace and kindness; it simply means we shouldn't allow other people's bad habits to influence our character. On the other hand, godly friends have the potential to make a positive impact. "As iron sharpens iron, so a man sharpens the countenance of his friend" (Proverbs 27:17). When two pieces of iron are rubbed together, one sharpens and shapes the other.[6] Being around godly people who are mature in their faith and growing as Christians will help us thrive.

> *Father, give me Your wisdom in choosing friends. Lead me to people who have the character to be a positive influence, and help me be a positive influence for others.*

41

Serving God does make us
very rich, if we are satisfied
with what we have.

1 TIMOTHY 6:6 NCV

When people think of riches, they most often associate the term with financial wealth. In Paul's letter to his young protégé, Timothy, he pointed out that serving God does make us rich, but not in the way most people think (1 Timothy 6:6). Paul's point was that a relationship with God provides things for us that money can't buy. When we enjoy close fellowship with God, it produces contentment and spiritual riches. People can count themselves truly wealthy when they are content with what they have. Contentment isn't obtained by reaching a specific financial status. It's possible to be a billionaire and be in constant want of new things, and it's possible to have a meager income and be satisfied. Our relationship with Christ is the only thing that will ultimately meet our needs and satisfy our desires. A relationship with Jesus brings contentment and makes us truly rich.

Jesus, I pray for a relationship with You that satisfies my every need and desire. Help me to be content with what I have and find complete satisfaction in You.

42

A sound heart is life
to the body,
but envy is rottenness
to the bones.

PROVERBS 14:30

*A*s humans we tend to compare ourselves to other people, and when we do, the outcome is never desirable. If we determine we are doing better than someone else, there is a risk for pride and self-righteousness. If we see someone else excelling and outpacing us, there is a good chance we will envy them. The writer of Proverbs warned against envy and went as far as to describe it as "rottenness to the bones" (14:30). Toxic attitudes impact our physical health. When our heart is at peace, it contributes to our well-being, but when we are distraught over what someone else has that we lack, it will eventually be harmful to our bodies. Envy is an indicator that we are more concerned with personal status than with God's glory. As Christ-followers, our goal is to use what we have to bring God glory. Envy and comparing ourselves to others are stumbling blocks that should be avoided.

Father, give me eyes to see the role I have as Your child and servant. Help me avoid the trap of comparison and envying others. I'm grateful for the ways You have blessed me.

43

Do you not know that
you are the temple of
God and that the Spirit
of God dwells in you?

1 CORINTHIANS 3:16

The Bible is full of important truths we are prone to forget. In today's reading, Paul raised a question in his letter to the church at Corinth and asked if they were aware that the Holy Spirit dwelled in them. If we aren't mindful of the Holy Spirit's presence, we will fail to draw strength from Him, and as a result, we will walk in the flesh rather than the Spirit (Romans 8:8–9). The Spirit is present to help us in our weaknesses. The Holy Spirit helps, teaches, guides, convicts, and empowers us to glorify God (John 14:17; 16:8–13). Every Christ-follower is a temple of the living God and is holy. Jesus knew we would need help. That's why He sent us a Helper, the Holy Spirit (John 16:7; Acts 2:1–4). As believers, we need to be mindful of the Holy Spirit's presence and continually rely on His strength.

> *Lord, forgive me for the times I have ignored the presence of the Holy Spirit. Please give me increased mindfulness of His presence so that I will obey His promptings.*

44

"Come to me, all who labor and are heavy laden, and I will give you rest. Take my yoke upon you, and learn from me, for I am gentle and lowly in heart, and you will find rest for your souls."

MATTHEW 11:28–29 ESV

If we want to have ample energy to do all the things God has called us to, it's important to avoid overbooking our schedule. Often we say yes to things that might be good but aren't necessarily God's will for how we should spend our time. To be sure, Jesus calls us to serve Him, but today's reading teaches He doesn't call us to do everything. In the New Testament era, people knew that a yoke was used to go across the neck of two farm animals and connect them to the plow they would pull. A yoke didn't completely eliminate the weight, but it distributed it so that neither animal was overly burdened with the task. In the same way, all of us have workloads we are required to carry, but Jesus comes alongside us and carries the burdens that are too heavy for us to carry on our own. It's impossible to have a flourishing spiritual life if we are chronically exhausted. What do you need to let go of to create margin?

Jesus, I am grateful for Your compassion. Teach me to say yes when I need to, and give me the wisdom to say no when I should.

45

My soul shall be satisfied as
with marrow and fatness,
and my mouth shall praise
You with joyful lips.

PSALM 63:5

here we direct our praise has much to teach us about the state of our heart. Boasting in our own abilities and accomplishments signals that we are relying on our own strength and have placed our hope in ourselves. In the same way, if we chronically direct our praise to other people or organizations, there's a good chance we are putting our confidence in things of this world. In today's reading, we see David placing full confidence in God. Like all of us, David had failed time and again. He'd also been sorely disappointed by other people. David knew he couldn't place His ultimate hope for fulfillment in anyone but God. He knew God wouldn't disappoint him, and he could say with confidence, "Because Your lovingkindness is better than life, my lips shall praise You" (Psalm 63:3). Is worship a regular part of your life? If so, where and to whom do you direct your praise?

> *Father, I want to be someone who praises You all the days of my life. Like David, I place my confidence and trust in You.*

46

Forgetting what is behind
and straining toward what
is ahead, I press on toward
the goal to win the prize for
which God has called me
heavenward in Christ Jesus.

PHILIPPIANS 3:13–14 NIV

istraction is a threat to our spiritual growth. In Paul's letter to the Philippians, he readily admitted he had not reached all of his goals, but he remained motivated and focused on pursuing them. In today's passage, Paul likened his spiritual journey to a race. All runners realize they must fix their eyes on the finish line. Watching the sidelines or looking back is a risk that will cause an athlete to lose focus and possibly stumble. To make progress in any area, we must possess extreme focus, and our spiritual lives are no exception. Paul noted that he disregarded what was behind him. We need to disregard our past, too, both good and bad. Christ-followers cannot coast on previous victories, nor can they be paralyzed by past sins. To make progress, we must direct our thoughts ahead. The Christian life calls for perseverance, and we must "press on" in all circumstances, with the goal of Christlikeness (Philippians 3:12, 14 NIV).

> *Jesus, I ask You to increase my focus. Give me a single-minded goal to know You well and to become increasingly more like You. Help me to ignore the distractions and press forward.*

47

Wine is a mocker,
strong drink is a brawler,
and whoever is led
astray by it is not wise.

PROVERBS 20:1

$\mathcal{I}$f we want to have a strong spiritual life, there are certain pitfalls to be avoided. Addiction comes in a variety of shapes and forms, and none of us are immune to temptation. In today's passage, the writer of Proverbs warned about the dangers of being led astray by alcohol consumption. According to statistics, in the United States more than fifteen million over the age of eighteen struggle with alcoholism. Approximately eighty-eight thousand people each year in America die from alcohol-related causes.[7] It's impossible to enjoy close fellowship with God if we are enslaved to alcohol or anything else. God intends for His people to be free from anything that oppresses us. The threat of addiction is something all believers need to be vigilant about guarding against. Paul instructed his readers, "Stand fast therefore in the liberty by which Christ has made us free, and do not be entangled again with a yoke of bondage" (Galatians 5:1).

Father, help me avoid any addiction that enslaves and oppresses. Teach me to stand firm in the liberty Jesus has won for me.

48

God said, "I give you every
seed-bearing plant on the
face of the whole earth
and every tree that has
fruit with seed in it. They
will be yours for food."

GENESIS 1:29 NIV

It's no secret that medical experts are constantly encouraging people to eat more fruits and vegetables and less processed food. Research has shown time and again that the healthiest food for us to eat is grown in gardens and on farms and is minimally processed. Everything that God provides for us is good. When God commands us to avoid something in the Bible, it's not because He is holding out on us, but because it has the potential to cause us harm. Taking good care of our bodies calls for proper nutrition. Eating a healthy diet doesn't guarantee we will avoid sickness, but it's part of being good stewards of the body we have been given. If we eat a diet filled with junk food, we are courting medical problems. Although exercise and proper nutrition don't make us exempt from disease, they do lower our chances of avoiding some problems and give us the opportunity to feel our best.

> *Lord, help me to make wise eating choices that increase my energy and help me feel my best.*

49

My dear friend, I know
your soul is doing fine, and
I pray that you are doing
well in every way and that
your health is good.

3 JOHN V. 2 NCV

When the apostle John wrote a letter to his friend and beloved elder, Gaius, he opened the letter by mentioning his body and soul. John wrote, "Dear friend, I pray that you may enjoy good health and that all may go well with you, even as your soul is getting along well" (3 John v. 2 NIV). John had a strong desire for his friend to be in good health so he could avoid the struggle of medical problems and be free to serve God without distraction. John's attitude reflects God's concern for the physical well-being of His people.[8] In the Old Testament, dietary laws and even regulations about personal hygiene were put in place to help protect God's people from illness. We can be confident that God cares about our health and that we, too, should be people who take good care of our bodies.

> *God, thank You for being mindful of my physical ailments and caring for me. Please increase my wisdom in caring for my body and soul.*

50

He restores my soul;
He leads me in the paths
of righteousness
for His name's sake.

PSALM 23:3

*M*any of us are fascinated with home improvement and restoration projects. Cable television is filled with weekly shows that showcase home remodels and reveal stunning before-and-after pictures. Watching run-down homes being transformed into beautiful, new living spaces gives us hope that broken things can be restored and made beautiful again. In a way, these shows serve as metaphors for our spiritual lives. Spiritually speaking, we experience times when our souls are run-down and maybe even in shambles. Long seasons of hardship deplete our resources and leave us feeling empty. We might wonder if there is anything left to salvage. In today's reading, the psalmist revealed that the Lord is faithful to restore our souls. Psalm 23 expresses confidence in God's loving care. In the same way a shepherd cares for his sheep, so does Jesus care for His followers by leading, providing for, and protecting us. Our souls were not designed to be in shambles or empty but to be filled to the fullest measure.

Jesus, thank You for caring for me as a shepherd tends to his flock. Restore my soul. Leave no part of me empty. Fill me with You.

51

Your beauty should not come
from outward adornment,
such as elaborate hairstyles
and the wearing of gold
jewelry or fine clothes.
Rather, it should be that of
your inner self, the unfading
beauty of a gentle and quiet
spirit, which is of great
worth in God's sight.

1 PETER 3:3–4 NIV

*A*ccording to Scripture, godly women are created to have far more going for them than physical appearance. In today's passage, the apostle Peter was not forbidding women to tend to their outward appearance, but he was calling women to a greater depth. Women who are overly consumed with their physical appearance, and nothing else, tend to be considered shallow. All women have higher callings than simply being admired for their beauty. Physical beauty and modern fashions are temporary, but godly character lasts a lifetime and even impacts eternity. Peter was encouraging his female readers to pay attention to inner qualities and character, which are valued by God. In a beauty-driven culture, this calls for intentionality on our part. How does the time you spend tending to your appearance compare to the time you invest in your spiritual development? Our schedules reflect what matters most.

> Lord, I confess I am sometimes overly consumed with external things. Help me to take good care of my body without neglecting my spiritual life.

52

A merry heart goes
good, like medicine,
but a broken spirit
dries the bones.

PROVERBS 17:22

*O*ur emotions have an impact on our physical bodies. If we habitually allow our emotions to dictate our choices, our lives will be chaotic, so it's important to learn to manage our thoughts. In today's passage, the writer of Proverbs communicates to us that a merry heart is good for the body, but a broken spirit is detrimental to our physical health. Hard times can't be avoided, so it's crucial we keep a close rein on our thought life. When it comes to happiness, the most important factor is not our circumstances but our thoughts.[9] The good news is, we can reject negative thoughts and things that don't align with God's Word. One of the best ways to combat negative thinking is to fill our minds with the promises of Scripture. When we are tempted to think bad thoughts or entertain things that aren't true, we can interrupt those thoughts with the truths of God's Word.

Father, I pray I will be quick to interrupt negative thoughts with the truths of Scripture. Teach me to meditate on Your promises and life-giving truths.

53

Let each person examine
his own work, and then he
can take pride in himself
alone, and not compare
himself with someone else.

GALATIANS 6:4 CSB

Mature faith calls for self-examination. In Paul's letter to the church at Galatia, he taught that mature believers are to gently restore others who get caught up in sin. But Paul cautioned that a believer's first order of business is to examine her own life to be certain she is obedient to God. That doesn't mean any of us is without sin. The Bible teaches we all fall short of the glory of God (Romans 3:23). But Christ-followers who obey God's Word to the best of their ability, rely daily on God's grace, and are growing in wisdom and knowledge of God are the type of believers who are best equipped to help a person who stumbles. How often do you take an honest inventory of your relationship with God? When a believer stumbles, she needs mature believers to help her get back on the right track.

Father, I want to help others who are struggling. Give me a heart for those who have gotten off track. Use me to point other people back to You.

54

Make every effort to
supplement your faith
with virtue, and virtue with
knowledge, and knowledge
with self-control, and self-
control with steadfastness,
and steadfastness with
godliness, and godliness
with brotherly affection, and
brotherly affection with love.

2 PETER 1:5–7 ESV

To experience a healthy spiritual life, we need to guard against complacency. Complacency is seldom intentional, but it creeps in without us noticing. In today's passage, the apostle Peter listed qualities that a mature believer possesses in increasing measure. These traits don't represent a legalistic code of rules but are indicative of a transformed heart that is growing in Christlikeness. We won't become more like Jesus by attempting to be like Him, but as we spend time with Jesus, His character rubs off on us. When we engage in spiritual disciplines, such as Bible study, prayer, and worship, we put ourselves in a posture to be transformed by His grace. Spiritual growth is a gift from God, but it requires our participation. That's why Peter wrote, "Make every effort . . ." (2 Peter 1:5 ESV). We will never drift toward spiritual maturity. Close fellowship with God, vibrant faith, and a thriving spiritual life are endeavors that demand our attention.

> *Father, help me to guard against complacency and to be quick to sense its presence. I want my love for You to increase with each passing year as I mature in my faith.*

55

We . . . glory in our
sufferings, because we
know that suffering
produces perseverance;
perseverance, character;
and character, hope.

ROMANS 5:3–4 NIV

*I*n a fallen world, seasons of suffering are unavoidable. Medical problems, the loss of loved ones, financial woes, depression, broken relationships, loneliness, and anxiety are some of the most common culprits. During times of hardship, we often ask, "Why is this happening?" We won't always have the answers, but as Christians, we can be assured our suffering is never wasted. In God's infinite power, He is able to take our suffering and bring good. In today's passage, the apostle Paul told his readers that we can "glory" or rejoice in our suffering because God uses seasons of suffering to make us more like Jesus. When we are desperate, we are more likely to give God our undivided attention. It is during these times that God works in us to produce godly character. It's still an unpleasant process, but we can be confident our suffering won't last forever, and God will bring good from our hardest times.

Father, thank You that not one minute of my suffering is ever wasted. I long to be more like Jesus, so when hard times come, please help make me more like Him.

56

"Which of you by worrying can add one cubit to his stature? If you then are not able to do the least, why are you anxious for the rest? Consider the lilies, how they grow: they neither toil nor spin; and yet I say to you, even Solomon in all his glory was not arrayed like one of these."

LUKE 12:25–27

At some point, everyone struggles with worry. One day, when Jesus was speaking to His disciples, He brought up the topic of worry. In today's reading, Jesus asked if any of the disciples were able to change their circumstances or even add one hour to their lives by worrying. He was making the point that worry is ineffective. Then He shifted to the topic of faith. To illustrate His point, Jesus urged His disciples to consider the lilies of the field. Flowers don't worry or strive for anything, He said, yet God provides everything they need to bloom. In the same way, God's people are not to strive but to trust Him to provide. Worry is an indicator that we fear God won't come through for us, but time and again God has proven Himself faithful. If God provides for the lilies, Jesus argued, He will most certainly provide for His people.

Father, I confess I struggle with worry. When I can't see the final outcome, I fear You won't come through for me. Give me faith that exceeds my fear, and increase my trust in You.

57

God is my strength and
power, and He makes
my way perfect.

2 SAMUEL 22:33

*M*ental and physical exhaustion is a toxic combination that leaves us questioning if we can carry on at the pace that is expected of us. During times of extreme fatigue, it's hard to make good choices or to know which direction to take. King David was no stranger to these dilemmas. David spent a long and stressful season being chased by enemies who wanted to take his life before he could become king of Israel. God finally rescued David and brought him safely through the terrifying situation. Undoubtedly, David had experienced days when he was running low on energy and didn't know what to do. After David's ordeal, he said, "God is my strength and power, and He makes my way perfect" (2 Samuel 22:33). David didn't say that because he'd lived a life of ease. He had learned those truths in the trenches. It's during difficult times when our faith is stretched that we learn to rely on God.

Lord, thank You for replenishing my energy and strength. Help me to remember I am relying on Your resources and not my own, so there is never any reason for me to fear.

58

"My grace is sufficient for
you, for my power is made
perfect in weakness."

2 CORINTHIANS 12:9 NIV

The Scriptures don't provide the specifics, but we know that the apostle Paul struggled with what he referred to as a "thorn in [his] flesh" (2 Corinthians 12:7). Whatever the problem was, it was so bothersome to Paul he pleaded with God three times to remove it, but God refused. Instead, today's scripture tells us, God told Paul that His grace was sufficient and he needed to rely on God's power rather than his own. When God calls us to difficult seasons, He gives us the grace to persevere. God's grace gives us the power to be who He has called us to be and do the things He has called us to do no matter how challenging the circumstance. Sometimes it's tempting for us to worry about how we will make it in the days, weeks, months, and years to come. But God provides His grace at the exact time we need it and not a minute before. We can be confident God will provide at just the right time.

Jesus, thank You for always giving more grace. Teach me to live minute by minute in Your sustaining power. Help me to trust Your grace will come at the exact moment of need.

59

Now to him who is able to
do above and beyond all that
we ask or think according
to the power that works
in us—to him be glory in
the church and in Christ
Jesus to all generations.

EPHESIANS 3:20–21 CSB

*A*s human beings, we know that our thoughts, hopes, and expectations are limited. The Bible makes it clear that God's thoughts are higher than ours: "'For my thoughts are not your thoughts, and your ways are not my ways.' This is the LORD's declaration. 'For as heaven is higher than earth, so my ways are higher than your ways, and my thoughts than your thoughts'" (Isaiah 55:8–9 CSB). When we fail to understand what God is doing in a given situation, we can trust His ways are more informed than ours. As believers indwelt with the Holy Spirit, there is no limit to what God can do in our lives. It's our responsibility to keep moving forward in faith, trusting that God's capability is unlimited, His resources are incalculable, and He has a better plan for us than we could ever dream. Our task is to be patient and trust His goodness until we can see His plan unfold.

> *Father, You are capable of more than I could ask or imagine. I want Your will for my life and trust You to bring things to pass that I never would have dreamed.*

60

I will never forget
Your precepts,
for by them You have
given me life.

PSALM 119:93

A lot of people neglect soul-care, but if we want to grow spiritually, we will make it part of our daily routine. One of the primary ways we tend to our souls is through reading God's Word. In today's passage, the writer of Psalm 119 communicated the importance of God's Word and said he would never forget God's "precepts," which is another word for God's commands. The psalmist said, "For by them You have given me life" (v. 93). The Word of God revives and restores our souls. God's Word is different from any other form of communication. The writer of Hebrews described it as "living and powerful, and sharper than any two-edged sword, . . . discern[ing] of the thoughts and intents of the heart" (4:12). When we read the Holy Scriptures, we fellowship with the Author of life, and as we do, our hearts, minds, and souls are filled with the ways of God.

> *Father, thank You for the gift of the Holy Scriptures. Increase my understanding of Your Word, and help me to make soul-care a part of my daily routine.*

61

May grace and peace be
multiplied to you in the
knowledge of God and of
Jesus our Lord. His divine
power has granted to
us all things that pertain
to life and godliness.

2 PETER 1:2–3 ESV

*H*ave you ever needed something but lacked the resources to secure it? Frustrating, isn't it? It's tempting to fall into the trap of thinking, *If only I had _____, I could achieve success.* When it comes to our spiritual lives, we already have been gifted with everything we need. In today's reading, the apostle Peter assured his readers that God has blessed all believers with everything we need to live a godly life. We don't have to wait for additional provision, nor do we lack anything that is essential. Because of God's grace, our spiritual resources are more than enough to meet every need. Not only has God provided a way for our salvation, but He also gives us the grace to grow into mature believers. This is a theme that Paul spoke of as well: "God is able to make all grace abound to you, so that having all sufficiency in all things at all times, you may abound in every good work" (2 Corinthians 9:8 ESV).

> *God, thank You for gifting me with every spiritual resource I need to live a godly life. Teach me to be mindful of Your grace and to rely on it wholeheartedly.*

62

He has made everything beautiful in its time. Also He has put eternity in their hearts, except that no one can find out the work that God does from beginning to end.

ECCLESIASTES 3:11

As we age, it's common to think about our legacy. We all hope to live long and productive lives, but even then it's hard for us to contemplate the fact that our time on this earth is limited. In today's reading, King Solomon shed some light on why this is true. Solomon wrote, "He has put eternity in their hearts" (Ecclesiastes 3:11). As human beings, we instinctively know there is more to this life than a typical life span of seventy to eighty years. We strive to live long lives because we innately understand we were built for more. We know this because God has put eternity in our hearts. A time will come when our life in this world will be over, but that doesn't mean we will cease to exist. Rather, we will either spend eternity with God, or we will be separated from Him. God has gifted us with this life to prepare for the next.

> *Father, I know my time on this earth is limited. Teach me to live with wisdom so I can make the best use of my life.*

63

Do your best to live in
peace with everyone.

ROMANS 12:18 NCV

If we are inclined, we can find a reason to be irritated seven days a week. All people have flaws, and if we make it a habit, we become experts at pointing out other people's shortcomings. But a critical spirit leads to a miserable life. If our relationships are in constant turmoil, there's a good chance we are contributing to the negativity. Instead of pointing out everything that is wrong, our relationships will be healthier if we develop an eye for pointing out what people are doing right. The quality of our relationships has a strong influence on our degree of happiness. The apostle Paul encouraged his readers to try to live in peace with everyone. Even when both parties make an effort, that is not always possible, but as a general rule, if we try our best to have agreeable relationships, there's a good chance we will have genuine friendships and limited drama.

> Lord, please bless me with healthy friendships. Help me to be a good friend and someone who lives peaceably with other people.

64

We have troubles all around us, but we are not defeated. We do not know what to do, but we do not give up the hope of living. We are persecuted, but God does not leave us. We are hurt sometimes, but we are not destroyed.

2 CORINTHIANS 4:8–9 NCV

$\mathcal{G}$od intends for His people to be entirely dependent on Him. Human beings are not designed only to attempt what we are confident we can accomplish in our own effort. God created people to live by faith and to rely on His strength and power. In today's passage, Paul described the troubles he was experiencing as an apostle. These verses demonstrate a paradox that is common in the Christian life. For instance, Paul had troubles, but he wasn't defeated. He didn't know what to do, yet he was hopeful. He was being persecuted, but God hadn't abandoned him. He was hurting but not destroyed. Despite Paul's suffering, he hadn't lost heart. In the midst of trials that test our faith, Christ-followers can be assured God will manifest His power and goodness. Our job is to take our needs to Him in prayer and trust that He will act.

> *Father, I am grateful that You have the power to see me through every difficulty. Help me to remember I am entirely dependent on You and I need never lose heart.*

65

The kingdom of God is not
eating and drinking, but
righteousness, peace, and
joy in the Holy Spirit.

ROMANS 14:17 CSB

Christians are not called to have a relationship with Jesus alone. Some of the greatest gifts of the Christian life are the relationships we develop with our brothers and sisters in Christ. In today's passage, Paul was communicating to his audience how to be sensitive to the needs of fellow Christians. Paul addressed the fact that under the new covenant we have more freedom in regard to what we eat and drink compared to the strict dietary laws of the Old Testament. But Paul urged Christians to be sensitive to other Christ-followers who choose to abstain from certain practices and not to cause weaker Christians to stumble. Our liberty is between God and us, but if weaker Christians see our actions, and we influence them in a negative manner, then we haven't acted in love. Paul pointed out there are far more important things to be enjoyed in the kingdom of God than just eating and drinking. At the heart of the Christian life is showing kindness and sensitivity to all.

Father, thank You for my brothers and sisters in the faith. Help me to be sensitive to their needs, and guard me against behavior that could make someone else stumble.

66

Run from anything that
stimulates youthful lusts.
Instead, pursue righteous
living, faithfulness, love,
and peace. Enjoy the
companionship of those
who call on the Lord
with pure hearts.

2 TIMOTHY 2:22 NLT

*A*dolescent temptations often follow us into adulthood. When Paul wrote to Timothy, he was thirty years Timothy's senior.[10] It's likely that as a younger man, Timothy was still struggling with temptations common to young people. Sexual desires outside the context of marriage, pride, excessive ambition, and a craving for notoriety and wealth are typical struggles for young people. Paul urged Timothy to run from anything that stirs youthful lusts. Mature Christians make a lifelong habit of avoiding temptations that lead to sin. Instead of succumbing to the sins of our youth, Paul instructed believers to pursue righteous living, faithfulness, love, and peace with people who have a like-minded goal of spiritual growth and maturity. When we are surrounded by friends who have the same desires for a close relationship with God, we can draw encouragement and enjoy fellowship with them, and that will help in our battle with temptation.

Father, help me to be mindful of triggers that tempt me to sin. Give me the wisdom to run from anything that might cause me to stumble, and surround me with people who long for a vibrant faith.

67

There is one who speaks like
the piercings of a sword,
but the tongue of the
wise promotes health.

PROVERBS 12:18

*N*othing reveals our spiritual maturity or lack of it like our tongue. In the Scriptures God repeatedly warns His people to be careful with words. In his letter to the church at Ephesus, Paul wrote, "Let no corrupt word proceed out of your mouth, but what is good for necessary edification, that it may impart grace to the hearers" (Ephesians 4:29). In the life of the believer, there is no place for gossip, unnecessary criticism, crude talk, flattery, mocking, or insults. Our words have the capability of doing terrible damage. In today's passage, the writer of Proverbs compared harsh words to piercing like a sword, while a wisely spoken word promotes health. The Scriptures teach that no human being has the ability to tame his tongue (James 3:8). The good news is, nothing is impossible for God, and He is well able to tame our tongues. A well-controlled tongue should be a constant prayer request because it's God's will for us to control our speech.

> *Father, I confess I have sinned with my speech. I cannot tame my tongue, but nothing is too hard for You. Remove from me the things You find offensive.*

68

If anyone is in Christ, he is
a new creation; old things
have passed away; behold,
all things have become new.

2 CORINTHIANS. 5:17

Regardless of our sin history, the Bible teaches that God's mercy and grace are powerful enough to wipe the slate clean for even the worst sinner. At the time of our salvation, we each become a new creation in Christ. The transformation isn't limited to the miracle of our salvation but also includes the lifelong process of becoming more like Jesus. As we mature, our old way of thinking, habits, desires, and plans change. Some things we used to love become repulsive to us, while some things we used to find repulsive we come to love. Along with our new salvation, God plants within us new loves, desires, goals, and dreams. Our fresh perspective helps us to grow into the people God intends for us to be, aids us in our battle with sin, and helps us to conform in likeness to Jesus.

Father, thank You for making me a new creation. Help turn my new desires, loves, goals, and inclinations into reality. Empower me to grow into the person You desire me to be.

69

With You is the
fountain of life;
in Your light we see light.

PSALM 36:9

*M*ost of us want to live our lives to the fullest, but sometimes we don't know how. In today's passage, the phrase "fountain of life" (Psalm 36:9) refers to everything that refreshes and sustains life.[11] The phrase "see light" literally means to experience life. The psalmist's point is that God is the Source of life, and it's impossible to live a full life apart from Him. Because of Christ's sacrifice on the cross, sinful human beings have the opportunity to be reconciled to God. This means we can enjoy abundant life now and eternal life in the future. Jesus said, "I am the light of the world. Whoever follows me will never walk in darkness, but will have the light of life" (John 8:12 NIV). Apart from Jesus, we remain in darkness. Author and apologist C. S. Lewis wrote, "God cannot give us happiness and peace apart from Himself, because it is not there. There is no such thing."[12]

Lord, please give me the peace and happiness that can only be found in You. I long to live my life to the fullest. Teach me to walk in the light of Christ.

70

I know how to live when I am poor, and I know how to live when I have plenty. I have learned the secret of being happy at any time in everything that happens, when I have enough to eat and when I go hungry, when I have more than I need and when I do not have enough.

PHILIPPIANS 4:12 NCV

*C*ontentment is valuable and learned by being subjected to a variety of situations. We'll never learn contentment by experiencing only plenty or always experiencing lack, but by being exposed to both.[13] The depth of our character is revealed in how we deal with both poverty and riches. We must ask, "Would I be content if I were forced to live in poverty?" In the same way, if we suddenly experienced a windfall of money, "Would wealth corrupt my character?" In today's passage, the apostle Paul revealed he had learned the secret to being content in every situation. His relationship with God was the source of Paul's contentment, and so his contentment remained stable and independent of all circumstances. Paul wasn't asserting that he was so strong that he couldn't be impacted by outward circumstances, but instead, he could say, "I can do all things through Christ, because he gives me strength" (Philippians 4:13 NCV).

> *Jesus, I don't want my happiness to be contingent on outside circumstances. Help me to find my contentment and joy in You.*

71

May the God of hope fill
you with all joy and peace as
you believe so that you may
overflow with hope by the
power of the Holy Spirit.

ROMANS 15:13 CSB

When we are tempted to quit, hope is the fuel that keeps us going. The secular view of hope isn't much help to us because it is passive in nature and not much more than wishful thinking. For instance, we hope it doesn't rain on our vacation, or we hope for the best. But biblical hope isn't passive; it is motivated by faith. Biblical hope can be defined as anticipation that God will do as He has promised, and it possesses confidence in His divine promises.[14] In today's reading, the apostle Paul referred to God as the "God of hope." God's people are called to be filled with hope and to live with our eyes open, anticipating that we will see God's promises come to pass. As we live in faithful expectation that God will do as He has promised, we experience joy and peace. Doubt and cynicism are not characteristics associated with a mature believer in Christ. God intends for us to be people of hope.

> *Father, I believe Your promises and wait with anxious anticipation that I will see many of them come to pass in this lifetime. Fill me with Your hope as I trust in Your promises.*

72

You will show me
the path of life;
in Your presence is
fullness of joy;
at Your right hand are
pleasures forevermore.

PSALM 16:11

King David was a flawed man who succumbed to grievous sins, but there is no doubting His love for God. Psalm 16 is a declaration of David's confidence in the Lord and his contentment in Him. David acknowledged every good thing he possessed had come from God: "I say to the LORD, 'You are my Lord; I have no good apart from you'" (v. 2 ESV). Like David, as we grow in our faith, we enjoy God in increasing measure. As our fellowship with God becomes stronger, we come to know Him better, and as a result, love Him more. David enjoyed his relationship with God and anticipated spending eternity with Him (v. 11). If we want to experience a growing spiritual life, we will make our relationship with Jesus the greatest priority of our lives. Our relationship with God influences every aspect of our life, and the degree of our joy or lack of it rises and falls with our relationship with Christ.

> Lord, I want to know You well and be as close to You as I can be. Like David, I long for You to make my heart glad and to rejoice in Your presence.

73

Get rid of all bitterness,
rage, anger, harsh words,
and slander, as well as all
types of evil behavior.

EPHESIANS 4:31 NLT

*H*ave you ever noticed how quickly junk accumulates in our homes? It's not uncommon to clean out closets and donate or throw away belongings we no longer use. In the same way, our spiritual lives accumulate things that no longer fit. As believers, we must do a constant inventory and get rid of things that aren't appropriate for a child of God. In today's passage, Paul included a list of traits that have no place in the life of a Christian. To "get rid of" means to no longer let these traits be a part of our daily life. Ridding our lives of these tendencies will demand prayer and pleading with God for the grace to obey. But when God calls His people to do something, we can be confident He will give us the grace we need to obey. Our role is to confess and repent of the behavior and to seek God's strength to move forward in righteousness.

> *Father, I don't want to keep anything in my life that is offensive to You. Give me the desire and strength to get rid of old behavior that doesn't align with who I am in Christ.*

74

Keep a close watch on
yourself and on the teaching.
Persist in this, for by so
doing you will save both
yourself and your hearers.

1 TIMOTHY 4:16 ESV

*I*t might seem strange, but as we grow in spiritual maturity, we become more aware of our inclination to sin. In Paul's first letter to Timothy, he instructed the young servant of God to keep a close watch on himself and his teaching. Paul took special care to tell Timothy to "persist in this" (4:16 ESV). No matter how long we have been a Christian, or how close we are to God, we will always be vulnerable to sin. As believers, we struggle with our flesh, the Enemy, and living in a world engulfed in sin. There will never be a time when we can assume we are immune to temptation. The apostle Peter warned, "Be sober-minded; be watchful. Your adversary the devil prowls around like a roaring lion, seeking someone to devour" (1 Peter 5:8 ESV). Self-examination is a routine part of possessing mature faith, and it's wise for us to surround ourselves with mature believers who can redirect us if we get off track.

> *Father, please grant me discernment, and give me a nudge when I start to get off track. Help me have the strength to persevere in my faith until You call me home.*

75

For the LORD God is
a sun and shield;
the LORD will give
grace and glory;
no good thing will
He withhold
from those who
walk uprightly.

PSALM 84:11

arly on in our Christian faith, there is a tendency to fear we might miss out if we follow Jesus. It's not uncommon for new Christians to question if obedience to Christ will limit their fun. In today's passage, the psalmist used a metaphor that compares the Lord to a sun and a shield. In other words, God serves as our light and our protection. The psalmist went on to explain that God gives us both grace and glory, and He doesn't hold back anything of value to those who possess genuine faith. As Christians, we have no reason to fear we are missing out. The only things that God forbids us to have are things that bring harm or have the potential to destroy. When our goal is to live in the center of the Lord's will, God is not tightfisted in His blessings; He is more than willing to provide everything that is good.

> *God, thank You for Your willingness to bless Your people. Please lavish Your grace on me so I can live the way You intended.*

76

Pleasant words are
like a honeycomb,
sweetness to the soul and
health to the bones.

PROVERBS 16:24

*O*ur words have the potential to be a blessing to those in our sphere of influence. We may not realize it, but on any given day, we speak to people who are in desperate need of encouragement, kindness, and affirmation. In today's passage, the writer of Proverbs was comparing pleasant words to honeycomb and describing a good word as "sweetness to the soul and health to the bones." We are prone to forget the power of our speech. But words have the capability of helping someone in a time of need. There's a good chance you can remember a kind word spoken to you that you have never forgotten. In the same way, many of us have had unkind words spoken to us that are impossible to forget. How would people closest to you describe your speech? We can choose to speak words that encourage and never harm. Our words carry influence, and we need to choose them with intentionality.

> *Father, fill my mouth with words of encouragement, kindness, grace, and truth. Help me to speak words that help and never hurt.*

77

We have this treasure in jars
of clay to show that this all-
surpassing power is from
God and not from us.

2 CORINTHIANS 4:7 NIV

*I*t's human nature to attempt to hide our weaknesses, but God is well aware of our fragility and is not put off by our shortcomings. In the ancient world, the phrase "jars of clay" (2 Corinthians 4:7 NIV) was a common metaphor used to describe human weakness.[15] In today's passage, the apostle Paul was describing the struggles he and his ministry team were facing as they took the gospel to a lost world. Paul communicated to his audience that human weaknesses demonstrate that it is God's power that works in us, rather than our own, to accomplish our callings. Paul was not discouraged by his own limitations but rather encouraged because the power of God rested on him. God does not call us to deny our weaknesses and pull ourselves up by our bootstraps. Instead, He instructs His people to acknowledge our weaknesses and to trust Him to do what we can't do for ourselves.

Father, I struggle with self-righteousness and wanting to do things on my own. Teach me to acknowledge my weakness and to trust Your power and not my own.

78

Great peace have those who love Your law, and nothing causes them to stumble.

PSALM 119:165

It has been said that a Bible that is falling apart usually belongs to someone who isn't. This pithy saying is reflective of today's passage because the psalmist was describing those who love God's Word as people who experience great peace and aren't inclined to stumble. When we spend time in God's Word, our thoughts shift from the troubles and temptations of this world to the ways of God. As we read the Scriptures, our thoughts are renewed, and our eyes are directed to the Lord's power. The prophet Isaiah wrote, "You will keep him in perfect peace, whose mind is stayed on You, because he trusts in You" (26:3). If we want to be people who are growing in our faith and experiencing fellowship with God, we will be people who spend time in God's Word. There is no substitute for the Scriptures, and we will never waste a moment we spend in the Bible.

> *Father, please give me a deep love for Your Word and a strong desire to study Your Scriptures. Increase my knowledge and understanding, and help me to obey Your commands.*

79

Then, because so many
people were coming and
going that they did not even
have a chance to eat, he
said to them, "Come with
me by yourselves to a quiet
place and get some rest."

MARK 6:31 NIV

*D*uring His earthly ministry, Jesus kept a busy schedule. Everywhere He turned, people approached Him in desperate need. Despite the constant demands on His time and attention, Jesus habitually made time to slip away from the crowds and go to quiet places where He could refill and spend time with the Father (Luke 5:16). In our fast-paced culture, it's not uncommon for us to have excessive demands on our schedule. Raising children, investing in our careers, the responsibilities of home life, tending to our physical health, and meeting social obligations all take time and energy. Keeping up with this pace means we must take time to refill. If Jesus, the all-powerful Son of God, found it necessary to spend time alone with God, then how much more should we? Spending time alone with God is not selfish, but rather the only way we can give our best to every endeavor.

Father, I desperately need time with You to refill my reserves. Give me the wisdom to make this a priority. Help me live with an intentionality that puts my relationship with You above all things.

80

My flesh and my heart fail;
but God is the strength of my
heart and my portion forever.

PSALM 73:26

*T*aking good care of our bodies is essential, but no matter how diligently we tend to our health, if we live long enough, a time arrives when our bodies inevitably fail us. In today's passage, the psalmist noted a time was coming when his flesh and heart might fail, but God never would. As we age or suffer illness, we experience a sense of vulnerability, because we aren't sure how things will unfold. If we aren't mindful of God's faithfulness, we become fearful of what the future might hold. God is our strength in every season of life, and from the womb to the tomb, He meets every need. The psalmist wrote, "You will guide me with Your counsel, and afterward receive me to glory" (Psalm 73:24). God sees us through every phase of life, and when our days on earth come to an end, He will see us safely home.

> *Father, I put my full trust in You during every season of life. Thank You for the knowledge that even if my body fails me, You never will.*

81

And let the peace that
comes from Christ rule
in your hearts. For as
members of one body you
are called to live in peace.
And always be thankful.

COLOSSIANS 3:15 NLT

I n modern times, we often associate peace with a lack of conflict. But in the New Testament, peace is often referred to as a personal state of being and can also refer to a characteristic that results from having a relationship with God.[16] Defined that way, peace isn't contingent on outward circumstances or lack of conflict but depends solely on our relationship with Christ. In today's passage, the apostle Paul was encouraging his readers to let the peace of Christ rule their hearts. According to Paul, God's people are called to live in peace. A right relationship with God produces peace in our hearts and serves as an anchor to our souls. Even when our outside circumstances are crumbling, we can experience the peace that Paul described. Gratitude is an important aspect of living in peace because it trains our eyes to look for the ways God has blessed us. Instead of focusing on what we lack, our thoughts are directed to our blessings.

Jesus, I want my heart to be filled with the peace that comes from You. Help me to remember to live with thanksgiving.

82

I have been crucified with
Christ. It is no longer I who
live, but Christ who lives in
me. And the life I now live in
the flesh I live by faith in the
Son of God, who loved me
and gave himself for me.

GALATIANS 2:20 ESV

*B*efore our salvation, our agenda is to live for self-exalting desires. The people we were before we trusted Christ as our Savior possessed different goals, motives, and desires. But at the time of our salvation, there is a shift in our allegiance. Rather than living to glorify ourselves and satisfying our own desires, we now live for Christ and His will. In today's passage, the apostle Paul spoke of his former self being "crucified with Christ." To be sure, Paul's distinct personality remained intact, but his motives were different. After his salvation, the driving factor in Paul's life became Jesus. Day by day and moment by moment, Paul lived by faith in Christ and depended on His power for spiritual effectiveness. The change in allegiance is reflective of what it means to "die to self." Later, in the book of Galatians, Paul wrote, "Those who belong to Christ Jesus have crucified the flesh with its passions and desires" (5:24 NIV).

> *Father, help me to disregard my own agenda and live in the center of Your will. Teach me to live by faith in Jesus and trust His plan for my life.*

83

"I am the resurrection
and the life. The one who
believes in me will live,
even though they die; and
whoever lives by believing
in me will never die."

JOHN 11:25–26 NIV

$\mathcal{I}$t's easy to get so caught up in the cares of this world we spend little time thinking about the life to come. Christians need to contemplate eternity. The Bible teaches that our souls will never cease to exist, and we will spend eternity either with God or apart from Him.

In the gospel of John, Jesus went to see His friends Mary and Martha, who were grieving the death of their brother, Lazarus (John 11:17–20). Before raising Lazarus from the dead, Jesus spoke with Martha and told her about the life to come. Jesus shared that He is the resurrection and the life and that even though we die, those of us who trust Him as our Savior will never die but will experience eternal life. Jesus said, "Whoever lives by believing in me will never die. Do you believe this?" (v. 26 NIV). The question Jesus asked Martha is a question we must ask ourselves: "Do you believe this?" What we truly believe will impact our actions and influence both the present and the future to come.

Father, please give me an eternal perspective. Empower me to spend my days in a way that is reflective of the reality that I will spend eternity with You.

84

When He had sent the
multitudes away, He
went up on the mountain
by Himself to pray.

MATTHEW 14:23

*D*uring His time on earth, Jesus experienced the soul-draining impact of living in a fallen world. In the gospel of Matthew, Jesus received the devastating news that John the Baptist had been murdered. Upon hearing the news, Jesus wasn't able to grieve because a crowd of people was following Him and wanted Him to heal the sick among them (Matthew 14:12–14). After a long day of ministering and feeding five thousand, Jesus sent the people away and went up to the mountain to pray (v. 23). It's notable that there were still plenty of people who wanted to see Jesus. The crowd didn't disperse on its own; Jesus had to send them on their way. Jesus guarded His prayer time, even if it meant disappointing people. After a mentally and physically exhausting time of ministry, Jesus knew prayer was what He needed. Regardless of our schedule, we must set boundaries to protect our time with God. Prayer is vital to our faith, and without it, we will be ineffective.

> *Jesus, I acknowledge I can do nothing apart from You. Help me devote myself to prayer, and give me the wisdom to set boundaries that guard my time with You.*

85

My soul thirsts for God,
for the living God.

PSALM 42:2

*D*id you ever drink something that failed to quench your thirst and left you even more parched than before? Spiritually speaking, we do it all the time. In today's passage, the psalmist communicated he was thirsty for the living God. He understood it was God he was longing for, but we don't always make that connection. Often, when we feel a longing in our souls, we attempt to quench our thirst with something we think will make us fulfilled. Common counterfeits we turn to are food, consumerism, addictions, relationships, and entertainment. The problem is, those things don't really quench our thirst. As believers, we have the privilege of being in a relationship with the living God. We don't have to settle for counterfeits that cannot satisfy. Jesus said, "I am the bread of life. He who comes to Me shall never hunger, and he who believes in Me shall never thirst" (John 6:35).

> *Jesus, You are the only One who can fill the longing in my soul. Give me wisdom to turn away from counterfeits that have no ability to satisfy me.*

86

We thank God! He gives
us the victory through
our Lord Jesus Christ.

1 CORINTHIANS 15:57 NCV

*I*magine standing before a judge in a court of law, knowing you were guilty and deserved a sentence of death. But before handing down the sentence, the judge announced your acquittal because someone else, an innocent person, had already served your sentence. In a simplified sense, that is the reality for those of us in Christ. Paul wrote, "For the wages of sin is death, but the gift of God is eternal life in Christ Jesus our Lord" (Romans 6:23). In light of this truth, gratitude should be a defining characteristic of every child of God. Apart from God's grace, we were defeated in sin and subject to the wrath of God. But in His mercy, God gave us victory through Jesus Christ, who took our penalty at Calvary (1 Corinthians 15:57). Although we were guilty of sin, God permitted all who believe in Christ to trade a life of sin for Christ's perfect record of obedience to the law (Romans 5:19). That's enough reason to praise God every day for the rest of our lives.

> *Jesus, You took the penalty I deserved and declared me not guilty. May gratitude be a defining characteristic of my life.*

87

Blessed is the man whose
strength is in You.

PSALM 84:5

I n the Old Testament, it was traditional for Jewish men to travel to Jerusalem three times each year to participate in annual feasts (Exodus 23:17). In Psalm 84 the writer described the beauty of God's temple and the privilege of making the pilgrimage to Jerusalem for worship. He wrote, "My soul longs, yes, even faints for the courts of the LORD; my heart and my flesh cry out for the living God" (Psalm 84:2). For many Jews, making the trip to Jerusalem was no easy task. The journey demanded time, effort, and physical stamina. But God's people are called to corporate worship, and God supplied strength and provision for the travelers to make the trip. As modern believers, we are no longer required to go on pilgrimage to Jerusalem three times each year, but we are called to gather with other believers to worship in biblical community.

Father, thank You for the privilege of worshiping with fellow believers. Help me to find my place in biblical community and to commit wholeheartedly to the local church.

Blessed are those who hunger
and thirst for righteousness,
for they will be filled.

MATTHEW 5:6 CSB

We make time for things that are most important. For instance, if our favorite music group or sports team is coming to town, there's a good chance we'll move mountains to attend. Or if we're training for a marathon, we'll be sure to do our long-distance runs. In the same way, when we long for a deeper spiritual life, we don't sit by, passively waiting for it to come, but we will do everything possible to experience it. In today's passage, Jesus was preaching His Sermon on the Mount, and He made the point that those who hunger and thirst for righteousness are not disappointed but find themselves satisfied. If we are hungering and thirsting for righteousness, we will put ourselves in a posture to receive. God always honors our eagerness to experience more of Him. The apostle James wrote, "Draw near to God and He will draw near to you" (James 4:8). We can be as close to God as we choose to be. If we long for a deeper relationship with Christ, our actions will demonstrate our desires.

> *Father, I want to know You as well as a human being is capable of knowing You. As I draw near to You, I trust Your promise that You will draw near to me.*

89

The way of the LORD is
strength for the upright,
but destruction will come
to the workers of iniquity.

PROVERBS 10:29

*A*s Christians, our best days are ahead of us. The Bible teaches that a time is coming when Christ-followers will be in the presence of God and experience eternal happiness. Every problem that tormented us in this world will have come to an end (Revelation 21:4). But a different kind of future awaits those who are evil. In today's passage, the writer of Proverbs said those who work iniquity have destruction ahead of them. In His Word, God has revealed a path for His people to follow. God's path is a place of security that leads to a future we can look forward to, filled with joy and peace beyond our wildest imagination. But those who choose to live a life apart from God travel on a different path, one that leads to destruction. It's good to remind ourselves that any sadness we experience on earth has an expiration date, and eternal joy awaits us.

God, thank You for revealing Your ways to us in Your Word. Help me to remember that my best days are ahead of me. Keep me on the path of righteousness that leads to Christ.

90

The Holy Spirit helps us in
our weakness. For example,
we don't know what God
wants us to pray for. But
the Holy Spirit prays for us
with groanings that cannot
be expressed in words.

ROMANS 8:26 NLT

*W*ithout exception, the most fruitful Christians are those committed to prayer. The apostle Paul instructed his readers, "Devote yourselves to prayer with an alert mind and a thankful heart" (Colossians 4:2 NLT). But if we are honest, sometimes we aren't sure how we should pray, or we might wonder if we are praying in alignment with God's will. Even the apostle Paul, who lived in close fellowship with God and boldly proclaimed the gospel, didn't always know the best way to pray. It's impossible for even the most faithful Christians to know God's purposes concerning every need or issue.[17] In today's reading, Paul provided reassurance that the Holy Spirit prays for us in our weaknesses. The Spirit prays for us in a way that is beyond our understanding, with groanings that are too deep for words. The Holy Spirit's prayers on our behalf don't mean we shouldn't pray ourselves, but we can have confidence that the third person of the Trinity is interceding for us with the Father.

> *Father, it is an honor to consider that the Holy Spirit prays on my behalf. I long for a vibrant prayer life. Help me to devote myself to prayer.*

91

Therefore my heart is glad,
and my glory rejoices;
my flesh also will rest in hope.

PSALM 16:9

On any given day, we can be as happy as we choose to be. Outward circumstances might threaten our mood, but if we keep our mind focused, we will have good reason to experience gladness every day. In today's reading, King David communicated that his heart was filled with gladness. Why did David have a happy heart? In the previous verse, he wrote, "I have set the LORD always before me; because He is at my right hand I shall not be moved" (Psalm 16:8). David had learned the secret of focusing his thoughts on his relationship with God. If we allow our happiness to depend on everything running smoothly, we will often find ourselves in a foul mood. But David's relationship with God was his greatest source of happiness, and that didn't change. We, too, have the opportunity to find our greatest happiness in God. And if we do, there's no reason we can't experience gladness as a way of life.

Father, I don't want my circumstances to dictate my mood. I ask for a happy heart that finds my greatest joy in my relationship with You.

92

There remains therefore a
rest for the people of God.

HEBREWS 4:9

*A*t Calvary, where Jesus hung on the cross, the last words He uttered before giving up His spirit were, "It is finished!" (John 19:30). Those three words proclaimed that He had completed the mission the Father had sent Him to accomplish. Jesus had taken the penalty for the sins of humankind, and the debt was paid in full. As believers, this reality should come as a relief to us. In today's passage, the writer of Hebrews was speaking of rest for the people of God. Because of Christ's work on the cross, those of us who follow Jesus as Lord can cease from striving and rest in Christ's sacrifice on our behalf. Jesus has provided everything we need to be reconciled to the Father. Even our best works cannot save us because we are saved only by grace through faith in Christ (Ephesians 2:8–9). It is true that all believers will be characterized by good works because God's people are indwelt with God's Spirit. But good works are evidence of our salvation, not the means of it. In Christ, we find rest.

Jesus, thank You that my salvation was secured completely by Your work and not my own.

93

"Behold, I make all
things new."

REVELATION 21:5

$\mathcal{A}$re you weary of bad news and reports of evil occurring in our hometowns and places around the globe? We live in an era of 24/7 news, with stories of violence and corruption continually bombarding our news feeds. It's not uncommon for a well-informed citizen to consume a steady diet of disturbing news. But Christians aren't called to bury our heads in the sand and ignore world events. Even in the midst of troubling reports and heart-sinking news, we can be encouraged about the future. The book of Revelation tells of a time coming on the kingdom calendar when the evil things in this world will be no longer. Jesus says, "Behold, I make all things new" (21:5). God will not permit evil deeds to go on forever. We can look to the future with confidence, knowing Jesus has promised that all sadness, evil, and suffering will come to an end.

Lord, I anticipate the day when all suffering is over, and evil will be no more. Until that day comes, allow me to live as Your light in a dark world.

94

God is our refuge
and strength,
a very present help in trouble.

PSALM 46:1

When dangerous weather is approaching, meteorologists instruct those in the path of the storm to go to safe places. A place of shelter might be a basement or an inner room on a bottom floor where there is protection from damaging winds and flying debris. Storms come in a variety of forms, and it's possible that Psalm 46 was written around the time the Assyrian army invaded and surrounded Jerusalem. The people of Jerusalem had seen their share of trouble, and they were no strangers to hardship. In today's passage, the psalmist identified God as the source of strength, refuge, and help during times of trouble. As believers living on this side of the cross, we are not exempt from the storms of life. But during times of trouble, God is our safe place. We can go to Him ever-confident that we will find peace and refuge in the power of His presence.

> *Father, I'm grateful You will never abandon me in times of trouble. I run to You when the storms of life threaten my safety and peace.*

95

Denying ungodliness and
worldly lusts, we should live
soberly, righteously, and
godly in the present age.

TITUS 2:12

*E*ach generation has its own set of challenges. But God has assigned each one of us the place and time frame in which we live (Acts 17:26). In today's passage, the apostle Paul was instructing his readers to deny ungodliness and worldly lusts and live sober and righteous lives in our present age. Some temptations of the present age differ from even a generation ago. The internet and social media have introduced both new opportunities and new challenges for believers. In an age of unlimited information and never-ending distractions, believers now have to take greater measures to stay focused on tasks and avoid negative influences. Christ-followers are navigating new territory and learning how to handle social platforms with humility, kindness, and grace. Regardless of the times we live in, Christians are called to live godly lives. Instead of being heavily influenced by the times, God's people are to make an impact on the generation in which we live for the better.

> *Father, I ask for wisdom to know how to live righteously in my generation. Help me to navigate the times with humility, grace, and kindness.*

96

O God, my heart is steadfast;
I will sing and give praise.

PSALM 108:1

od is worthy of all praise and glory. As recipients of God's love, grace, and provision, a lifestyle of praise and glory to God is our only appropriate response. All human beings are image bearers of God (Genesis 1:27). Although we cannot increase His glory, when our lives reflect His attributes, other people see God's goodness, and we exalt His reputation on earth. Offering praise to God in prayers and song is another way we give God glory. Both our words and our lives can bring glory to God. Practically speaking, to glorify God means to obey Him and proclaim His goodness in word and deed. Bringing glory to God should be the motivation of every believer. Our sinful natures long to bring glory to ourselves. But when the Holy Spirit leads us, our lives will reflect the glory of God, and we will desire to make Him known.

> *Father, I confess I have sinned by attempting to bring glory to myself. I am made to bring glory to You. I pray my life will reflect Your goodness and enhance Your reputation on earth.*

97

Let anyone who is thirsty
come. Let anyone who
desires drink freely from
the water of life.

REVELATION 22:17 NLT

The Christian life is not an exclusive club reserved for specific members. The gospel of Jesus Christ issues an invitation to all sinners. In today's passage, the apostle John made it clear the invitation to come to Jesus is for anyone who is thirsty for the water of life. In the Bible, thirst is a familiar metaphor that represents spiritual need. The prophet Isaiah wrote, "Is anyone thirsty? Come and drink—even if you have no money! Come, take your choice of wine or milk—it's all free!" (Isaiah 55:1 NLT). To come to Jesus, the only thing required is need. As believers, it's our calling to share the gospel with those who have yet to hear. We don't need a theology degree to share our faith, and we don't have to know all the answers. Our personal testimonies are powerful. It's often been said, "Evangelism is just one beggar telling another where to get food."[18]

Jesus, thank You for giving me the water of life. Give me opportunities to tell others what You have done for me. I pray I will be quick to share the gospel with those who need to hear.

98

Do not be wise in
your own eyes;
fear the LORD and
depart from evil.
It will be health to your flesh,
and strength to your bones.

PROVERBS 3:7–8

*A*ccording to the book of Proverbs, godly wisdom will guard our lives and promotes a lifestyle that benefits our body. Many times, if we use sound judgment and godly wisdom, we avoid many of the mishaps that plague the unwise. Bad choices cause untold stress on our mental health and hardship on our bodies. It's true that godly people suffer, but those who walk in the ways of God avoid the ultimate consequences of sin. There is no need for a wise person to be beset with anxiety because he can be confident he has made the best choices and can trust God with the outcome. A lifestyle of godly living avoids sinful habits that wreak havoc on our bodies. Not only are God's ways beneficial to our spiritual lives, but they are the best option for our physical, emotional, and mental health.

> *Father, thank You for caring for every aspect of my being. Your way of living promotes health in my body, soul, and mind.*

99

My soul shall be
joyful in the Lᴏʀᴅ;
it shall rejoice in His salvation.

PSALM 35:9

We have the freedom to choose our thoughts. None of us is immune to hardship, and most of us have survived things that hurt us deeply. But regardless of our past, what Christ has done for us is greater than what anyone else has done against us. As believers, our relationship with Christ can and should be the defining characteristic of our life. In today's passage, the psalmist defined the predominant theme he would dwell on: "My soul shall be joyful in the LORD; it shall rejoice in His salvation" (Psalm 35:9). Our souls are impacted by our thoughts. When our minds are set on the person and work of Jesus Christ, our souls will be filled with joy. What is the predominant theme of your thoughts? What steps can you take to be intentional about your thought life? For Christ-followers, the reality of our salvation and all we have in Christ gives us plenty of soul-stirring truths to contemplate.

Jesus, help me manage my thoughts. Make Your goodness the predominant theme in my mind. Teach me to rejoice in my salvation and all I have in You.

100

I will be glad you rejoice in
Your mercy, for You have
considered my trouble;
You have known my soul in
adversities, and have not
shut me up into the hand
of the enemy; You have set
my feet in a wide place.

PSALM 31:7–8

*A*t any given time, God knows the state of our hearts, minds, and souls. We never have to wonder if God knows what is going on or if He understands our trouble. In today's passage, King David acknowledged that God had considered his troubles and showed him mercy. David was in a tight spot, surrounded by enemies on every side. He called out to God, "In You, O LORD, I put my trust; let me never be ashamed; deliver me in Your righteousness" (Psalm 31:1). God delivered David from the enemies who planned to inflict harm. He rescued him from the tight spot he was in and set his feet in a wide place. God is intimately aware of every situation. When we are facing problems, we can be confident God understands the dynamics even better than we do. Like David's, our role is to call out to God and trust that He will act on our behalf.

Father, thank You for being aware of every situation. You are never aloof to my troubles. I ask You to rescue me from every threat and set my feet in a wide space.

Notes

CHAPTER 2

1. John MacArthur, *The MacArthur New Testament Commentary: Ephesians* (Chicago: Moody, 1986), 63.

CHAPTER 3

2. "Stress Is Killing You," Mastersdegreeonline.org, American Institute of Stress website, accessed March 12, 2019, https://www.stress.org/stress-is-killing-you/.

CHAPTER 24

3. President's Council on Sports, Fitness & Nutrition, "Facts & Statistics: Physical Activity," HHS.gov, last reviewed January 6, 2017, https://www.hhs.gov/fitness/resource-center/facts-and-statistics/index.html.

CHAPTER 32

4. John MacArthur, *The John MacArthur New Testament Commentary: Ephesians,* (Chicago: Moody, 1986), 248.

CHAPTER 34

5. Alexandra Sifferlin, "More Than Two Thirds of Americans Are Overweight or Obese," *Time*, June 22, 2015, http://time.com/3929990/americans-overweight-obese/.

CHAPTER 40

6. Max Anders, *Holman Old Testament Commentary: Proverbs* (Nashville: B&H, 2005), 116.

CHAPTER 47

7. National Institute on Alcohol Abuse and Alcoholism, "Alcohol Facts and Statistics," NIH, updated August 2018, https://www.niaaa.nih.gov/alcohol-health/overview-alcohol-consumption/alcohol-facts-and-statistics.

CHAPTER 49

8. John MacArthur, *The MacArthur New Testament Commentary: 1–3 John* (Chicago: Moody, 2007), 245.

CHAPTER 52

9. Max Anders, *Holman Old Testament Commentary: Proverbs* (Nashville: B&H, 2005), 338.

CHAPTER 66

10. John MacArthur, *The MacArthur New Testament Commentary: 2 Timothy* (Chicago: Moody, 1995), 93.

CHAPTER 69

11. ESV Study Bible (Wheaton, IL: Crossway, 2008), 982n.
12. C. S. Lewis, *Mere Christianity* (New York: Harper Collins, 1952), 50.

CHAPTER 70

13. D. A. Carson, *Basics for Believers: An Exposition of Philippians* (Grand Rapids: Baker Academic, 1996), 118–19.

CHAPTER 71

14. David Noel Freedman, *Eerdmans Dictionary of the Bible* (Grand Rapids: Eerdmans, 2000), 605.

CHAPTER 77

15. ESV Study Bible (Wheaton, IL: Crossway, 2005), 2228n.

CHAPTER 81

16. David Noel Freedman, *Dictionary of the Bible* (Grand Rapids: Eerdmans, 2000), 1022.

CHAPTER 90

17. John MacArthur, *The MacArthur New Testament Commentary: Romans 1–8* (Chicago: Moody, 1991), 466–67.

CHAPTER 97

18. Delos Miles, *Introduction to Evangelism* (Nashville: Broadman Press, 1983), 37.

My Favorite Bible Verses